Flamingos

Written by Hannah Reed

Flying Start
to Literacy®

Contents

Introduction

Millions of flamingos live on this lake.

The lake has food for them to eat. And it is a good place for them to build their nests and raise their chicks.

Most animals could not live on this lake, because there is a lot of salt in the water. But flamingos can live here.

Chapter 1: What they look like

The shape of a flamingo's body helps it to find food.

Legs and necks

Flamingos find food in water. They use their long legs to walk in the water to look for food.

Their long necks help them to reach down into the water to get food.

Webbed feet

Flamingos have webbed feet. This helps them to walk in mud.

When they walk in the water, their feet stir up the plants and animals that live in the mud. The flamingos can then eat the plants and animals.

Beaks

A flamingo's beak helps it to get food.
A flamingo uses its beak to scoop food
from the water.

Flamingos put their heads in the water to look for food. They sift plants and animals from the water to eat.

Wings

Flamingos have large, strong wings. When flamingos want to fly, they run and flap their wings. This helps them to get off the ground and into the air.

When they are flying, flamingos stretch their necks out in front and their legs behind.

Chapter 2:
Getting food

Sometimes, the wind makes waves on the lake where the flamingos live. When this happens, flamingos can't find food. To stop the waves, the flamingos stand together in a large group.

When the waves move between the flamingos' legs, the waves get smaller and smaller. In the middle of the flock, there are no waves and the flamingos can find food. Flamingos take turns at being on the edge of the flock and in the middle.

Water to drink

Flamingos cannot drink the water in
this lake, because it has lots of salt in it.
They drink fresh water from creeks and
rivers near the lake.

Sometimes, the only fresh water they can find comes out of the ground. This water can be very hot. Most animals cannot drink hot water, but flamingos can.

Chapter 3:
Raising their young

Flamingo parents build a nest in the mud. Then the female lays one egg. Both parents look after the nest and the egg.

They take turns sitting on the egg
to keep it warm. It takes more than
26 days for the egg to hatch.

Growing up

The chick pecks its way out of the egg.

When the chick has hatched, both parents look after it. A chick stays in its nest for up to 12 days.

While it is in the nest, its mother and father feed it.

Both the mother and father can make milk in their throats. They feed this milk to their chick.

When the chick leaves the nest, it stays
with the other chicks in a large group.
This keeps the chick safe while its
parents are away.

The parents feed the chick until it is
about 11 weeks old. Then it can
feed itself.

Flamingo chicks have grey feathers. When the chicks are about two years old, their feathers become pink or orange. The colour comes from the small animals flamingos eat.

Conclusion

Flamingos are amazing birds. They can live in salt lakes where other animals cannot live. But flamingos can – they can find food and raise their young in these places.

Index